Children'

MARY CADOGAN

MEREHURST

LONDON

Contents

Managing Editor: Janet Illsley
Photographer: James Murphy
Designer: Sue Storey
Food Stylist: Mary Cadogan
Photographic Stylist: Sarah Wiley
Typeset by Angel Graphics
Colour separation by J. Film Process Limited, Thailand
Printed in Italy by New Interlitho S.p.A.

First published 1990 by Merehurst Ltd,
Ferry House, 51/57 Lacy Road, Putney, London SW15 1PR
Reprinted 1991

© Merehurst Ltd

ISBN: 1 85391 134 8 (Cased)
ISBN: 1 85391 210 7 (Paperback)

NOTES

All spoon measures are level: 1 tablespoon = 15ml spoon;
1 teaspoon = 5ml spoon.

Introduction

A party is a magical, eagerly awaited time for children, but for the organiser an element of fear and trepidation usually sets in. There is never enough time to cook the food, organise games, do the shopping, stuff the party bags and blow up endless balloons. The answer is to keep everything simple, and to do as much as possible before the day.

Younger children usually enjoy lots of organised games and all the old favourites go down well. The over sixes, however, often prefer a bit more free time to play with the new toys or engage in some imaginative play acting. A swimming, farm or other activity party is always popular, and has the added advantage of being away from home, particularly if space is a problem. Games, food and prizes can also be geared to the party theme.

Party food must be easy to eat. For the younger ones, offer plenty of mouthful-sized morsels. The food can look very exciting with little extra effort – try pasties disguised as dinosaurs and a patchwork quilt of tiny sandwiches. Homemade fast food such as monster burgers and devilish dogs are just right for older guests.

All of the recipes in this book – including the party cakes – are devised to give maximum applause for minimum effort. Most of the cakes can be iced in less than an hour and freeze well, minus some decorations. Remember to buy extra bits to avoid squabbles over who has the lolly on the clown's hat, or the necklace in the treasure chest.

My own children were the chief tasters for this book, along with many of their friends who miraculously appeared when the food did! Recipes were adapted and re-tested in the light of their highly critical comments. I hope the results make your next party a great success.

Mary Cadogan

Pizza Toasties

If your party is for older children, provide them with a selection of ingredients, such as olives, salami, sliced peppers etc, so they can make up their own pizza toppings.

397g (14oz) can chopped
tomatoes, drained
1 tablespoon tomato purée
(paste)
salt and pepper
1 teaspoon dried oregano

125g (4oz) Mozzarella cheese
125g (4oz) sliced ham
4 wholemeal bread rolls
60g (2oz/½ cup) grated
Cheddar cheese

1 Place the tomatoes in a small saucepan with the tomato purée (paste), salt, pepper and oregano. Simmer, covered, for 5 minutes, stirring occasionally, until thick and pulpy.
2 Cut the Mozzarella and ham into cubes. Halve the rolls and toast them on both sides. Spread each cut side with the tomato mixture, then sprinkle with Mozzarella, ham and Cheddar. Grill for 2-3 minutes, until the topping is bubbling and lightly browned. *Makes 8.*

Pitta Pockets

Cocktail pittas make perfect party food and can be filled with all kinds of tasty morsels.

1 carrot
½ green pepper
4-6 slices salami

4-6 slices ham
mayonnaise for spreading
1 packet cocktail pitta breads

1 Peel carrot and cut into thin sticks. Cut the pepper into thin strips. Cut the slices of salami and ham in half and spread with a little mayonnaise. Place a carrot or pepper strip on each piece of meat and roll up.
2 Preheat the grill to medium and grill the pitta breads until they are warm. Split and fill with the prepared meats. Serve warm or cold. *Serves 6-8.*

Sesame Chicken Bites

The chicken pieces can be added to the batter and kept chilled for up to 2 hours until you are ready to cook them.

375g (12oz) boneless chicken breasts, cut into cubes
salt and pepper
125g (4oz/1 cup) self-raising flour

2 tablespoons toasted sesame seeds
185ml (6 fl oz/3/4 cup) water
oil for deep-frying
tomato ketchup to serve

1 Season the chicken cubes. Mix the flour, sesame seeds and a little salt in a bowl, then gradually stir in the water to form a smooth batter. Add the chicken and stir to coat each piece completely.
2 Heat the oil to 180C (350F), or until a little batter dropped into the oil rises and starts to brown immediately. Add a few chicken pieces and fry for 2-3 minutes until golden brown. Remove with a slotted spoon and drain well on kitchen paper; keep warm while you cook the remainder.
3 Serve warm, with ketchup for dipping. *Serves 8.*

Mexican Dip

1 ripe avocado
3 tablespoon Greek yogurt
1 tablespoon lemon juice
1/2 teaspoon paprika
salt and pepper to taste

TO SERVE:
tortilla chips
cauliflower flowerets
carrot sticks
button mushrooms
cucumber slices
cherry tomatoes

1 Halve and stone the avocado. Scoop the flesh into a blender or food processor and add the yogurt, lemon juice, paprika, salt and pepper. Blend until smooth.
2 Turn the dip into a serving dish and serve with the tortilla chips and vegetables for dipping. *Serves 6-8.*

Monster Burgers

These burgers are great for a small tea party. You can always get the diners to attach features to their own burgers – it's amazing how many expressions can be made!

500g (1lb) lean minced beef
1 tablespoon chopped parsley
1 tablespoon soy sauce
salt and pepper
4 burger baps
2 cheese slices
1 tablespoon oil

8 button mushrooms, stalks
* removed*
8 frozen peas
¼ red pepper
few lettuce leaves
1 tablespoon tomato ketchup

1 Place the beef, parsley, soy sauce, salt and pepper in a bowl and mix with your hands until all the ingredients are evenly distributed. Divide into 4 portions and shape into burgers. Split the baps in half.

2 Cook the burgers under a preheated grill for 12-15 minutes, turning once. Towards the end of the cooking time, toast the cut sides of the buns.

3 Meanwhile, cut each cheese slice in half, then halve each piece lengthwise in a zig-zag pattern. Heat the oil in a small pan and fry the mushrooms until cooked. Cook the peas in simmering water until tender; drain. Cut the pepper into short strips.

4 Place the burgers in the buns, tucking in some lettuce on either side. Place the mushrooms, cup-side up, on top, with a pea in each cup for the eyes. Arrange 2 zig-zag cheese slices on each burger for teeth. Add red pepper strips for eyebrows and a blob of ketchup for a tongue. Serve hot, with extra tomato ketchup. *Serves 4.*

Devilish Dogs

Hot dogs are popular party food – adding faces makes them much more fun.

4 long thin sausages
2 tomatoes
2 slices cucumber
1 slice cheese

4 long granary rolls
1 box cress
tomato ketchup to serve

1 Cook the sausages under a preheated medium grill, turning frequently, until well cooked, about 15 minutes. Cut each tomato into 4 wedges. Cut cucumber slices into quarters. Halve the cheese slice, then halve each piece diagonally.
2 Split the rolls in half. Put a sausage in each one and place a piece of cheese on top, to resemble a tongue. Tuck some cress into each end of the rolls.
3 Place the hot dogs on plates and position tomato quarters and cucumber pieces on top of each for eyes. Serve with tomato ketchup. *Serves 4.*

Tomato Eyes

A great favourite with children – when spooky food is called for.

250g (8oz) cherry tomatoes
salt
125g (4oz) soft cream cheese

1-2 teaspoons milk (optional)
¼ green pepper, diced

1 Cut tops off the tomatoes and scoop out seeds and flesh using a teaspoon handle. Sprinkle with a little salt and leave to drain upside down on a plate for 30 minutes.
2 Beat the cream cheese with a wooden spoon until smooth, adding a little milk if it is very stiff. Place in a piping bag fitted with a small star tube.
3 Place the tomatoes upright on a serving plate and pipe in the cheese. Top each with a pepper cube. *Serves 6-8.*

Treasure Bags

Ideal for pirates and other adventurers, these lightly spiced filo pastry pouches make a welcome change from sausage rolls.

8 sheets filo pastry
60g (2oz) butter, melted
FILLING:
1 tablespoon oil
1 small onion, finely chopped
1 small potato, grated
125g (4oz) frozen mixed
　　vegetables

1 teaspoon ground cumin
1 teaspoon ground coriander
2 teaspoons lemon juice
salt and pepper
TO FINISH:
8 chives

1 First make the filling: heat the oil in a small pan, add the onion and fry gently until softened but not browned; about 5 minutes. Add the potato and fry for a further 5 minutes. Add the mixed vegetables, spices, lemon juice, salt and pepper to taste. Cook gently, stirring, for 5-6 minutes, until the potato is softened. Leave to cool.

2 Preheat the oven to 190C (375F/Gas 5). Unwrap one sheet of filo, keeping the others covered as you work to prevent them drying out. Brush half the sheet with melted butter and fold in half. Brush again with butter and pile some filling into the centre. Gather up the edges of the pastry, to form a pouch, pinching them together to seal. Place on a greased baking sheet. Make the remaining pouches in the same way.

3 Brush the pouches with the remaining butter and bake in the preheated oven for 15 minutes until the pastry is crisp and golden brown. Tie a chive around each treasure bag and serve warm. *Makes 8.*

Devilled Bones

750g (1½lb) pork spare ribs
4 tablespoons soft brown sugar
2 tablespoons soy sauce

3 tablespoons tomato ketchup
3 tablespoons orange juice
3 tablespoons wine vinegar

1 Preheat the oven to 180C (350F/Gas 4). Cut each rib into three equal pieces, using a strong knife, or get your butcher to do this. Cook the ribs under a preheated medium grill for 10 minutes, turning frequently, until lightly browned. Drain on kitchen paper and transfer to a roasting tin.
2 Mix all the remaining ingredients together and pour over the ribs. Turn them in the sauce until evenly coated. Bake for 30 minutes, turning twice, until they are richly golden. Allow to cool a little before serving. *Serves 4-6.*

Sausage Snails

250g (8oz/2 cups) self-raising
*   flour*
60g (2oz) margarine
90g (3oz/¾ cup) grated
*   Cheddar cheese*

7 tablespoons milk
Marmite or Vegemite for
*   spreading*
16 cocktail sausages

1 Preheat the oven to 200C (400F/Gas 6).
2 Place the flour in a mixing bowl and add the margarine in small pieces. Rub in using your fingertips, until the mixture resembles fine crumbs. Stir in half the cheese. Add the milk and mix to a soft dough.
3 Roll out to a 30 x 10 cm (12 x 4 inch) rectangle and spread with a thin layer of Marmite or Vegemite. Sprinkle with the remaining cheese and roll up from a long side, leaving the last 2.5 cm (1 inch) unrolled. Cut into 16 slices and lay on their sides on a lightly greased baking sheet. Tuck a sausage into each roll beside the unrolled piece of dough, to form the snail's head. Bake for 15 minutes until golden brown. Serve warm or cold. *Makes 16.*

Dinosaur Pasties

Dinosaurs are always a favourite with children, and these ones taste good too! The filling can be adapted as you wish: for example, you could use chopped ham and cheese, tuna and sweetcorn, or cooked mixed vegetables bound together with a little ketchup.

125g (4oz/1 cup) wholemeal
    flour
125g (4oz/1 cup) plain flour
60 g (2oz) butter or margarine
125ml (4 fl oz/½ cup) water
250g (8oz) herby sausages

60g (2oz/½ cup) grated Cheddar
    cheese
1 egg, beaten
1 small piece carrot
shredded lettuce
1 box cress

1 Preheat the oven to 200C (400F/Gas 6).

2 Mix the flours together in a bowl. Place the fat and water in a small saucepan and heat gently until the fat has melted. Add to the flours and mix quickly to form a soft dough. Turn out onto a floured surface and knead briefly until smooth.

3 Remove the skins from the sausages and chop the sausage meat roughly. Mix with the cheese and half the egg. Roll out the dough thinly and cut out eight 10cm (4 inch) circles; reserve the trimmings. Pile the filling into the centre of the pastry circles and dampen the edges. Draw opposite sides of the pastry up over the filling and press the edges together, crimping them between your fingers and thumb.

4 Transfer the pasties to the baking sheet and brush with some of the remaining beaten egg. Shape the pastry trimmings into heads and tails and attach to the pasties. Brush with egg and stick 2 small pieces of carrot into each head for eyes.

5 Bake in the preheated oven for 20 minutes, until crisp and golden brown. Serve warm or cold on a bed of shredded lettuce and cress. *Makes 8.*

Dinghy Rolls

196 (7oz) can tuna, drained
3 tablespoons mayonnaise
6 small bridge rolls
5 cm (2in) piece cucumber

½ red pepper, diced
24 savoury party sticks, eg
  Twiglets

1 Mash the tuna with the mayonnaise. Halve the rolls and spread with the tuna mayonnaise.
2 Slice the cucumber lengthwise to form rectangles. Half each one diagonally to make triangular sails. Thread onto cocktail sticks and top each with a pepper flag. Stick each sail into a roll and add savoury sticks for oars. *Makes 12.*

Wiggly Worms

These cheese pastries are really tasty. If you prefer, you can always roll out the dough and cut it into stars or circles.

185g (6oz/1½ cups) plain flour
pinch of salt
1 teaspoon mustard powder
125g (4oz) soft margarine, cut
  into small pieces

90g (3oz/¾ cup) grated Cheddar
  cheese
1 egg, beaten
2-3 teaspoons poppy seeds
2-3 teaspoons sesame seeds

1 Preheat the oven to 200C (400F/Gas 6). Mix together the flour, salt and mustard. Add the margarine and rub in using your fingertips until the mixture resembles fine crumbs.
2 Stir in the cheese, then add 2 tablespoons beaten egg and mix to a soft dough. Knead lightly on a floured surface until smooth. Pinch off small pieces of dough and roll into sausage shapes, about 10cm (4 inches) long. Place a little apart on a greased baking sheet and curve into worm shapes. Brush lightly with the remaining egg and sprinkle with poppy or sesame seeds.
3 Bake for 8-10 minutes until golden brown. Carefully transfer to a wire rack to cool. *Makes 50-60.*

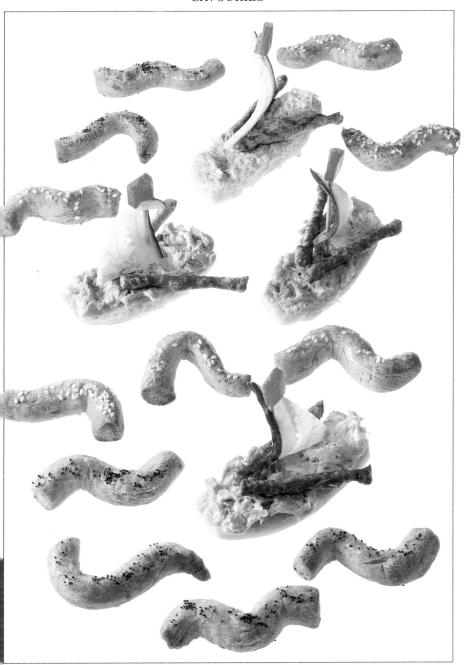

Hedgehog Rolls

Make these rolls in just one hour from start to finish. Most of the making and shaping can be done by the children with minimum help from an adult.

*250g (8oz/2 cups) white bread
    flour*
*250g (8oz/1¾ cups) wholemeal
    flour*
2 teaspoons easy-blend yeast
2 teaspoons salt

2 teaspoons sugar
*315ml (10 fl oz/1¼ cups) warm
    water*
beaten egg to glaze
16 currants

1 Preheat the oven to 220C (425F/Gas 7).

2 Mix together the flours, yeast, salt and sugar in a mixing bowl. Add the warm water all at once and mix quickly to form a soft dough. Turn out onto a floured surface and knead thoroughly for 10 minutes until the dough is smooth and no longer sticky.

3 Divide the dough into 8 equal pieces. Shape each into a ball and pull out to a point to form a snout. Place the rolls, a little apart, on the baking sheet.

4 Brush the rolls all over with beaten egg and apply currants for the eyes. Snip the body all over with scissors to form spines. Cover the rolls loosely with oiled polythene and leave to rise for about 30 minutes, until doubled in size, and the dough springs back when pressed.

5 Bake the rolls in the preheated oven for 15-18 minutes, until they are golden brown and sound hollow when tapped on the base. Cool on a wire rack. *Makes 8.*

Crunchy Bones

Here's another cunning way of serving sandwiches while pretending not to, as they are heavily disguised.

*4 rashers streaky bacon, rinds
  removed
1 small packet crisps*

*6 slices bread
butter for spreading*

1 Grill the bacon on both sides until very crisp. Drain well on kitchen paper and leave to cool. Crumble into very small pieces. Crush the crisps and mix with the bacon.
2 Remove the crusts from the bread and roll flat with a rolling pin. Spread the bread thinly with butter and sprinkle with the bacon mixture. Roll up tightly, then cut each roll in half. *Makes 12.*

Face Sandwiches

Supply plenty of ingredients for your guests to make their own sandwiches. I find they eat more of their own creations.

*6 slices white or brown bread
cheese spread for spreading
125g (4oz) cheese, grated
3 carrots, grated
sliced radishes*

*cherry tomatoes
cucumber slices, halved
red or green pepper strips
celery slices
cress*

1 Spread each slice of bread with cheese spread and place on individual plates. Arrange all the remaining ingredients on the table in small bowls or plates.
2 The cheese and carrot can be used for hair, beards and moustaches, and the other ingredients for features. *Serves 6.*

Patchwork Quilt

I find that children prefer lots of small morsels at a party, and these tasty cheese squares always appeal. You can use any cheeses you like, but make sure that their colours are strongly contrasting. My children are particularly keen on cheddar flavoured with pizza seasoning – a recent invention.

90g (3oz) Cheddar cheese
90g (3oz) Camembert
90g (3oz) Double Gloucester
  with chives
90g (3oz) flavoured Cheddar (eg
  red-veined)
4 slices wholemeal bread
cheese spread for spreading

TO GARNISH:
few radishes, sliced
small piece of cucumber, sliced
few black grapes, halved and
  seeded if necessary
parsley sprigs

1 Slice all the cheese thinly. Remove the crusts from the bread and spread the bread with cheese spread. Cover each slice of bread with a different cheese, then cut each slice into three each way, to give 9 squares of each variety.
2 Place a slice of radish on each Cheddar square, a quarter slice of cucumber on each Camembert square, half a black grape on each flavoured Cheddar square and a sprig of parsley on each double Gloucester square.
3 Arrange the cheese squares in rows of six on a flat plate or board, alternating colours to give a patchwork effect. Garnish with parsley. *Serves 4-6.*

Topsy Turvy Jellies

Jellies made from pure fruit juices are healthier and less sweet than packet jellies.

6 teaspoons powdered gelatine
4 tablespoons water
625ml (20 fl oz/2½ cups) red
  grape juice
625ml (20 fl oz/2½ cups) clear
  apple juice

few drops of green food
  colouring (optional)
250g (8oz) mixed fruit, eg
  seedless grapes, cherries,
  orange segments, apple cubes
4 mint sprigs

1 Dissolve 3 teaspoons gelatine in 2 tablespoons water. Add to the grape juice and stir well. Pour into 4 tall plastic glasses until half full. Carefully prop up in the fridge at a 45° angle and leave to set.
2 Dissolve the remaining gelatine in 2 tablespoons water. Stir into the apple juice, with the green colouring if using. When the grape jelly has set, stand the glasses upright and pour in the apple juice to within 2.5cm (1 inch) of the top. Return to the fridge to set.
3 Just before serving, arrange the fruit on the jellies and decorate with mint sprigs. *Serves 4.*

Chocolate Fruit Sticks

250g (8oz) strawberries
2 apples
2-3 plums

125g (4oz) seedless grapes
60g (2oz) cooking chocolate
1 grapefruit, halved

1 Hull the strawberries. Peel, core and chop the apples. Cut the plums into wedges, discarding stones.
2 Break up the chocolate and melt in a small bowl over hot water. Spear the fruit onto cocktail sticks and dip into the chocolate, turning to half-coat. Leave on a tray lined with non-stick paper until the chocolate has set.
3 Stick the fruit into the grapefruit halves. *Serves 6-8.*

Orangesnap Baskets

These edible baskets look very pretty filled with a selection of colourful fruits. You can also use them as containers for ice cream.

60g (2oz) butter
60g (2oz/¼ cup) caster sugar
90g (3oz/¼ cup) golden syrup
1 teaspoon orange juice
60g (2oz/½ cup) plain flour
½ teaspoon grated orange rind
1 red-skinned apple

1 orange
2 slices pineapple
125g (4oz) fresh or frozen
    raspberries
250g (8oz/1 cup) fromage frais
    or Greek yogurt
sugar to taste (optional)

1 Preheat the oven to 180C (350F/Gas 4). Line 3 baking sheets with non-stick paper.
2 Place the butter, sugar and syrup in a saucepan. Heat gently until the butter has melted and the sugar has dissolved. Remove from the heat and add the orange juice, flour and orange rind. Mix well, then leave to cool.
3 Place 4 teaspoonfuls of the mixture, well apart, on each baking sheet. Bake in the preheated oven, one sheet at a time, for 10-12 minutes, until the biscuits are spread flat and golden brown.
4 Leave the biscuits on the baking sheets for about 30 seconds, then remove with a palette knife and quickly place each one over an upturned tumbler, moulding them with your hands to form baskets. When set, carefully transfer to a wire rack and allow to cool. Make the remaining baskets in the same way.
5 Quarter, core and chop the apple. Peel the orange and cut into segments using a sharp knife, discarding all pith. Mix with the apple. Remove the skin and core from the pine-apple, then chop the flesh into cubes. Add to the other fruit with the raspberries.
6 Sweeten the fromage frais or yogurt with sugar to taste. Fill the baskets with the fruit and top each with a spoonful of fromage frais or yogurt. *Serves 12.*

Meringue Toadstools

These red-speckled toadstools are always popular with young children. To make mushrooms instead, dust the top of the meringues with cocoa powder instead of painting them with red dots, as illustrated.

2 egg whites
125g (4oz/¹/₂ cup) caster sugar
30g (1oz) cooking chocolate
red food colouring

60g (2oz/¹/₃ cup) desiccated
coconut (optional)
green food colouring (optional)

1 Preheat the oven to 140C (275F/Gas 1). Line several baking sheets with non-stick paper.
2 Place the egg whites in a clean bowl and whisk until very stiff and dry. Add 2 teaspoons sugar and whisk until the mixture is stiff and shiny. Add the remaining sugar, a little at a time, whisking well after each addition.
3 Spoon the meringue into a large piping bag fitted with a 1cm (¹/₂ in) plain nozzle. Pipe about 40 small rounded mounds, about 2.5cm (1 inch) across, onto the baking sheets to make the toadstool caps. Smooth the tops carefully with a knife if necessary. On another baking sheet, pipe 40 small blobs for the stalks.
4 Bake in the preheated oven for about 1 hour until the meringues can be removed easily from the paper. Transfer to a wire rack to cool.
5 Break up the chocolate and place in a bowl over a saucepan of hot water until melted. Place the toadstool caps upside down on a tray. Dip the end of each stalk into the chocolate and carefully fix each one onto a cap. Leave to set.
6 Colour the desiccated coconut with a few drops of green colouring if required. Spread over a serving plate to resemble grass. When the toadstools have set, paint tiny red spots on each cap, using a fine paint brush dipped in red food colouring. Place the toadstools in the grass. *Serves 40.*

Spider Buns

Make these buns for your next Hallowe'en party, if not before!

CAKE:
125g (4oz/1 cup) self-raising
   flour
125g (4oz/½ cup) caster sugar
125g (4oz) soft margarine
2 eggs
few drops of vanilla essence

1 teaspoon baking powder
ICING AND DECORATION:
185g (6oz/1 cup) icing sugar,
   sifted
2 tablespoons hot water
30g (1oz) plain (dark) chocolate
1 packet chocolate buttons

1 Preheat the oven to 180C (350F/Gas 4).
2 Place all the cake ingredients in a mixing bowl and beat with a wooden spoon, or using an electic mixer, for 2-3 minutes until light and fluffy. Divide between 18 paper cake cases. Bake in the preheated oven for 12-15 minutes, until risen and golden brown. Transfer to a wire rack to cool.
3 To make the icing, mix together the icing sugar and water until smooth. Melt the chocolate in a bowl over hot water. Place the chocolate in a greaseproof paper piping bag and snip of the end (or use a small piping bag fitted with a fine nozzle). Place 1 tablespoon icing in a similar piping bag; set aside.
4 Spread the icing on top of the cakes and place a chocolate button in the centre of each, for the spider. Use the melted chocolate to pipe 6 legs onto each spider. Use the reserved white icing to pipe on eyes. *Makes 18.*

Mini Christmas Puddings

Here is something children will love to help make, if you don't mind them getting a bit messy. To make cannon balls, shape the mixture into 24 balls and omit the icing; turn these into truffles by rolling in chocolate sugar strands.

90g (3oz/¼ cup) golden syrup
60g (2oz) butter or margarine
60g (2oz) plain (dark) chocolate,
  in pieces
155g (5oz) digestive biscuits
  (granitas)
2 tablespoons currants
30g (1oz/2 tablespoons) glacé
  cherries, finely chopped

ICING AND DECORATION:
60g (2oz/⅓ cup) icing sugar,
  sifted
1-2 teaspoons hot water
few strips of angelica, cut into
  leaves
few glacé cherries, chopped

1 Place the syrup, butter or margarine and chocolate in a saucepan. Heat gently, stirring occasionally, until melted to a smooth glossy sauce.

2 Put the biscuits between 2 sheets of greaseproof paper and crush with a rolling pin. Tip the biscuit crumbs into the saucepan, add the currants and glacé cherries and mix thoroughly. Leave the mixture to cool for a few minutes, until firm enough to handle.

3 Divide the mixture into 12 pieces and shape them into balls, using wet hands to make shaping easier. Place the balls in paper cake cases.

4 To make the icing, mix the icing sugar with enough water to make a smooth icing, thick enough to coat the back of a spoon. Spoon a little icing over each chocolate ball and top each with 3 angelica holly leaves and a few pieces of glacé cherry for berries. Leave until the icing has set. *Makes 12*.

Dice Cakes

Allow yourself a little extra time to ice these cakes – they are well worth the effort. I find it easier to place each cake on a large palette knife while applying the icing.

SPONGE:
2 eggs
60g (2oz/¼ cup) caster sugar
60g (2oz/½ cup) plain flour
30g (1oz) butter, melted
ICING AND DECORATION:
1 tablespoon apricot jam,
  warmed

185g (6oz) marzipan
375g (12oz/2¼ cups) icing
  sugar, sifted
3 tablespoons hot water
pink and yellow food colouring
185g (6oz) small jelly sweets

1 Preheat the oven to 180C (350F/Gas 4). Grease and base line a 20cm (8 inch) square cake tin.

2 Place the eggs and sugar in a bowl over a pan of hot water. Whisk using an electric beater for about 10 minutes, until the mixture is light and thick enough to leave a trail when the beaters are lifted.

3 Sift the flour over the mixture and fold in carefully, using a metal spoon. Slowly pour the melted butter into the mixture and fold in. Pour into the prepared cake tin and gently shake the tin to level the mixture. Bake in the pre-heated oven for 20-25 minutes, until golden brown and firm to the touch. Leave in the tin for 5 minutes, then turn out and cool on a wire rack.

4 Brush the top of the cake with jam. Roll out marzipan to a 20cm (8 inch) square and use to cover top of cake. Cut the cake into 5 equal strips each way, to give 25 squares.

5 To make the icing, mix the icing sugar and water together until smooth and glossy. Transfer half the icing to another bowl. Colour one portion pink and the other yellow with a few drops of each food colouring. Coat half of the cakes with pink icing and half with yellow icing. Place on a wire rack and decorate with jelly sweets to resemble dice. Leave until the icing has set, then place in paper cake cases. *Makes 25.*

Bird's Nests

Shredded wheat cereal gives a good looking nest, but if you prefer you can use cornflakes or bran flakes instead.

2 tablespoons clear honey
1 tablespoon soft brown sugar
125g (4oz) plain (dark)
  chocolate, in pieces
30g (1oz) butter or margarine

125g (4oz) shredded wheat
  cereal biscuits
30g (1oz) toasted sesame seeds
185g (6oz) sugar-coated
  chocolate eggs

1 Place the honey, sugar, chocolate and butter or margarine in a saucepan and heat gently, stirring occasionally, until smooth and glossy. Break up the cereal between your fingers and stir into the mixture with the sesame seeds.
2 Pile the mixture into 12 paper cake cases and make a slight hollow in the centre of each. Place a few eggs in each hollow. Leave to set. *Makes 12.*

Nutty Nuggets

These mouthful-sized treats can be made several days in advance and stored in an airtight container.

90g (3oz/1 cup) desiccated
  coconut
60g (2oz/½ cup) chopped
  walnuts
185g (6oz/1¼ cups) chopped
  dates

125g (4oz/1 cup) pre-soaked
  dried apricots, chopped
185g (6oz/1 cup) raisins
1 orange
30g (1oz) toasted sesame seeds
  for coating

1 Place the coconut, walnuts, dates, apricots and raisins in a blender. Peel and segment the orange, discarding all pith, then chop roughly and add to the blender. Blend until well mixed.
2 Form the mixture into small balls, about 2.5cm (1 inch) across, and roll in sesame seeds to coat. Place in paper sweet cases. *Makes 20-24.*

Window Biscuits

These biscuits look wonderful with the light shining through the 'glass'. Hang them up at the window, or make them at Christmas to hang on the tree.

125g (4oz) butter
125g (4oz/³⁄₄ cup) soft brown
*   sugar*
1 egg, beaten

250g (8oz/2 cups) plain flour
½ teaspoon baking powder
250g (8oz) boiled fruit sweets,
*   eg Glacier Fruits*

1 Preheat the oven to 180C (350F/Gas 4). Line 2 or 3 baking sheets with non-stick paper.
2 Place the butter and sugar in a mixing bowl and beat for 2-3 minutes, until the mixture is light and fluffy. Beat in the egg, then sift in the flour and baking powder and mix to a soft dough.
3 Turn the dough onto a lightly floured surface and knead briefly until smooth. Wrap in plastic wrap and chill for 20 minutes.
4 Roll out the dough on a lightly floured surface and cut out 7.5cm (3 inch) rounds, using a fluted cutter. Place the biscuits on the baking sheets. Carefully remove the centre of each biscuit, using a 5cm (2 inch) star cutter. Make a small hole in each biscuit if you are going to hang them up. Knead the trimmings together and use to make more biscuits.
5 Bake the biscuits in the preheated oven for 7 minutes, then remove from the oven and place two sweets of contrasting colours in the centre of each. Return to the oven for 3-5 minutes, until the sweets have melted to form the 'glass' in the windows.
6 Cool the biscuits on the trays for 2 minutes, then carefully transfer to a wire rack and allow to cool completely. Thread ribbon through the holes in the biscuits if you intend to hang them. *Makes 18-20.*

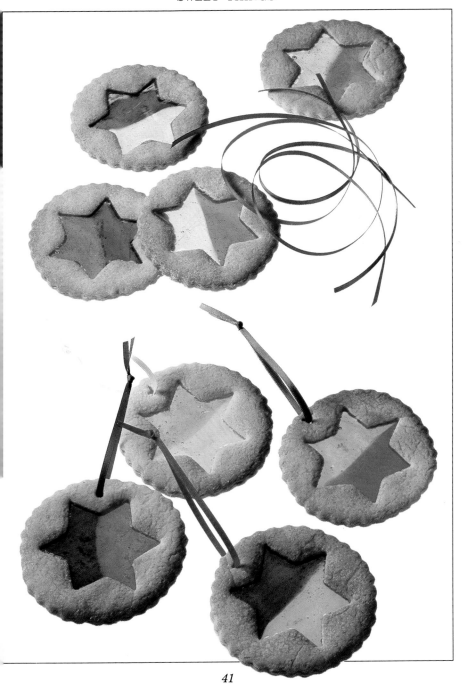

Astronaut Biscuits

The biscuits for these white-suited astronauts can be made several days in advance and stored in an airtight tin. Ice them on the day of the party.

250g (8oz/2 cups) plain flour
1 teaspoon mixed spice
1 teaspoon ground ginger
125g (4oz/¹/₃ cup) golden syrup
45g (1¹/₂oz) butter or margarine
3 tablespoons soft brown sugar
1 teaspoon bicarbonate of soda
1 teaspoon water

1 egg yolk
24-28 currants
TO DECORATE:
1 quantity moulding icing
  (page 79)
1 tablespoon warmed honey
silver balls

1 Preheat the oven to 190C (350F/Gas 5). Line a baking sheet with non-stick paper.
2 Sift the flour and spices into a mixing bowl. Place the syrup, butter or margarine and sugar in a small saucepan and heat gently until smooth.
3 Dissolve the bicarbonate of soda in the water. Add to the flour with the melted mixture and egg yolk. Mix to a soft dough and knead briefly. Wrap in plastic wrap and leave to rest in the refrigerator for 30 minutes.
4 Roll out the dough and cut out 12 to 14 men, using a gingerbread man cutter. Place, a little apart, on the baking sheet. Press on currants for eyes. Bake in the preheated oven for 6-8 minutes, until lightly browned. Cool on the baking sheet for 5 minutes, then carefully transfer to a wire rack and allow to cool completely.
5 Roll out the moulding icing on a board sprinkled with icing sugar, and cut out gingerbread men shapes, using the same cutter. Brush the body of each gingerbread biscuit with a little honey. Cut away the head of the icing figures and place the suits on the biscuit men. Use the trimmings to make helmets and attach with honey. Stick silver balls on the helmets and on the.suits, as buttons. *Makes 12-14.*

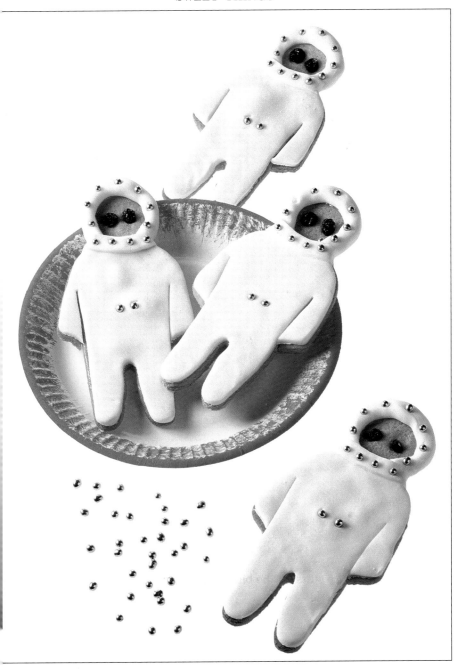

Tropical Crush

Serve this refreshing exotic drink at a summer children's party.

1 ripe mango
315ml (10 fl oz/1¼ cups)
pineapple juice
625ml (20 fl oz/2½ cups)
sparkling mineral water

2 slices pineapple
ice cubes to serve
4 cocktail umbrellas

1 Peel, halve and stone the mango. Chop the flesh and place in a blender. Blend until smooth, then press the pulp through a sieve into a jug to remove the fibres. Add the pineapple juice and stir well. Add the mineral water.
2 Remove the skin and core from 1 pineapple slice and chop finely; add to the jug. Cut the remaining slice of pineapple into 4 to 6 wedges. To serve, pour the drink into glasses, add ice cubes and decorate the rims with pineapple wedges and cocktail umbrellas. *Serves 4-6.*

Caribbean Froth

This milk shake looks wicked, but is packed with good things like milk and bananas. Try it with other fruits such as strawberries, peaches (skinned and stoned) and raspberries.

1 ripe banana
2 scoops vanilla ice cream
1 tablespoon caster sugar

625ml (20 fl oz/2½ cups)
cold milk
1 tablespoon toasted coconut

1 Peel and chop the banana and place in a blender with the ice cream, sugar and milk. Blend until smooth, then pour into glasses and sprinkle with coconut. Serve with bendy straws. *Serves 4.*

Lemonade Whizz

I make this drink all summer long for my children, who love its refreshing taste.

1 lemon
60g (2oz/¼ cup) caster sugar
ice cubes

940ml (30 fl oz/3¾ cups water)
lemon slices to serve

1 Scrub the lemon thoroughly and cut into small pieces. Place in a blender or food processor with the sugar, 6 ice cubes and a third of the water. Blend until the lemon is broken up, then strain into a jug. Return the pulp to the blender and add the remaining water. Blend for a few seconds, then strain the juice into the jug.
2 To serve, pour into tall glasses, top up with ice cubes and decorate with lemon slices. *Serves 6.*

Witches' Brew

Serve this ghoulish drink in a glass jug stuck all over with suitable spooky stickers or silver paper stars.

4 tablespoons granulated sugar
few drops of green food
  colouring
1 egg white, beaten
1 apple

90ml (3 fl oz/⅓ cup)
  blackcurrant cordial
940ml (30 fl oz/3¾ cups)
  sparkling mineral water

1 Place the sugar in a small bowl and add a few drops of green colouring. Stir until evenly coloured. Turn onto a plate. Pour the egg white onto a separate plate. Dip the rims of the glasses in the egg white, then into the sugar to coat evenly. Leave for 10 minutes to set.
2 Quarter and core the apple. Cut into small 'teeth-sized' pieces and place in a jug. Add the blackcurrant and water and stir well. Pour into the glasses, taking care to avoid the frosted rims, and serve. *Serves 6.*

Strawberry Thick Shake

Dessert whip comes in a variety of flavours and makes an instant thick shake which is always popular. Strawberry is a favourite flavour, and has a pretty colour too. A filling drink – ideal for hungry party goers!

69g (2.4oz) packet strawberry dessert whip
625ml (20 fl oz/2½ cups) cold milk

4 scoops vanilla ice cream
multicoloured sugar strands
4 cocktail umbrellas

1 Place the dessert whip and cold milk in a bowl and whisk with an electric whisk for 2-3 minutes, until it starts to thicken. Alternatively whizz in a blender until thickening.
2 Pour the mixture into 4 tall glasses or plastic beakers and place a scoop of ice cream on top of each serving. Sprinkle with coloured sugar strands and top with cocktail umbrellas. Serve immediately, with straws and spoons. *Serves 4.*

VARIATION: Replace strawberry dessert whip with banana flavoured whip. Top with vanilla or chocolate ice cream and chocolate or multicoloured sugar strands to serve.

Letter Biscuits

125g (4oz) butter
125g (4oz/¾ cup) soft brown
  sugar
1 egg, beaten

250g (8oz/2 cups) self-raising
  flour
½ teaspoon ground cinnamon
2 tablespoons caster sugar

1 Preheat the oven to 180C (350F/Gas 4).
2 Beat the butter and sugar together with a wooden spoon until light and fluffy, about 5 minutes. Beat in the egg, a little at a time. Sift in the flour and cinnamon and mix in lightly, using a metal spoon, to form a firm dough. Knead lightly on a floured surface. If the dough is too soft, cover with plastic wrap and chill for 20 minutes.
3 Pull off small pieces of dough and roll into sausages. Shape into letters, cutting as necessary. Place, a little apart, on lightly greased baking sheets and sprinkle with caster sugar. Bake for 15-20 minutes, until slightly risen and golden. Leave on the baking sheets for 1-2 minutes, then transfer to a wire rack to cool. *Makes about 24.*

Crunchy Clusters

125g (4oz/¾ cup) soft
  brown sugar
1 egg, beaten
90g (3oz/½ cup) raisins
60g (2oz/⅓ cup) glacé cherries,
  chopped
60 g (2oz/⅔ cup) porridge oats

60g (2oz/⅔ cup) desiccated
  coconut
60g (2oz/½ cup) chopped nuts
30g (1oz/2 tablespoons)
  sunflower seeds
½ teaspoon ground cinnamon
1 tablespoon sunflower oil

1 Preheat the oven to 160C (325F/Gas 3). Place the sugar and egg in a bowl and mix with a fork. Add the remaining ingredients and mix until evenly distributed.
2 Place heaped teaspoonfuls of the mixture, a little apart, on greased baking sheets. Bake for 15 minutes, until crisp and golden. Cool on the baking sheets for 5 minutes, then carefully transfer to a wire rack. *Makes 18-20.*

Meringue Gems

2 egg whites
125g (¾ cup/4oz) icing sugar,
  sifted

pink, orange and green food
  colourings
jelly diamonds

1 Place egg whites and icing sugar in a bowl over hot water and whisk with an electric whisk for about 5 minutes, until the mixture is thick and glossy and stands in stiff peaks. Remove from the heat and whisk for a further 2 minutes.
2 Divide mixture into 3 portions and add a few drops of colouring to each. Pipe into small stars on a baking sheet lined with non-stick paper. Press a jelly diamond on each.
3   Bake in the oven on the lowest setting for 1 hour, then leave to cool in oven. *Makes about 24.*

Peppermint Pigs

1 egg white
1 rounded tablespoon liquid
  glucose
few drops of pink food colouring
2 teaspoons peppermint essence

500g (1lb/3 cups) icing sugar,
  sifted
30g (1oz) plain (dark) chocolate,
  melted
24 silver balls

1 Place the egg white, glucose, pink colouring and peppermint in a bowl and beat lightly with a fork. Add the icing sugar gradually, mixing to a stiff dough. Knead on a surface dusted with icing sugar until smooth.
2 Divide the mixture into 12 pieces; keep covered.
3 To make a pig, divide a piece of dough in half, then halve one of these pieces again. Mould a barrel-shaped body with the large piece and a round head with a small piece. Use remaining piece to shape two floppy ears, a snub nose and 4 stubby feet. Attach features with a little melted chocolate. Mark a smile, using a knife, then press on 2 silver balls for eyes. Leave for several hours to dry. *Makes 12.*

Sarah

Father Christmas

The traditional Christmas cake is usually much too rich for young tastes. This jolly Santa makes a colourful centrepiece for the festive table.

5-egg basic cake mixture
  (page 79)
GLACÉ ICING:
185g (6oz/1 cup) icing sugar
1½ tablespoons hot water
yellow and pink food colourings
SOFT ICING:
500g (1lb/3 cups) icing sugar,
  sifted

250g (8oz) soft margarine
2 tablespoons milk
few drops of vanilla essence
TO FINISH:
red food colouring
assorted sweets
liquorice strips
desiccated coconut for
  sprinkling

1 Preheat the oven to 160C (325F/Gas 3). Divide the cake mixture between greased and base lined 20cm (8 inch) round and 15cm (6 inch) square cake tins, adding a little more than half to the round tin. Smooth the tops and bake for 30-35 minutes, until golden brown and firm to the touch. Turn out and cool on a wire rack.

2 To make the glacé icing, beat together the icing sugar and water until smooth and glossy. Add a few drops each of yellow and pink colouring to give a flesh tone. Cut the square cake in half diagonally, then attach to opposite sides of the round cake with a little icing, trimming the corners to fit. Place on a 43 x 25cm (17 x 10 inch) cake board. Spread the glacé icing over the round cake; leave to set.

3 Beat together the ingredients for the soft icing. Colour one third red and spread over one triangular cake for the hat.

4 Place the remaining soft icing in a piping bag fitted with a large star tube. Pipe a furry trim around the hat and a beard on the plain triangle. Pipe on eyebrows and position sweets for eyes and nose; liquorice strips for eyelashes and mouth. Paint on rosy cheeks with pink colouring. Sprinkle with desiccated coconut to represent snow. *Serves 20.*

Birthday Tea Table

For this pretty cake, you will need 4 wedding cake pillars and a thin 20cm (8 inch) cake board. Those of you who are artistic can shape small moulding icing figures to sit at the table.

3-egg basic cake mixture
  (page 79)
125g (4oz/¹/₃ cup) clear honey

1 quantity moulding icing
  (page 79)
sugar flowers
blue food colouring

1 Preheat the oven to 160C (325F/Gas 3). Half-fill 9 paper cake cases with cake mixture; spread the remainder in a greased and base lined 20cm (8 inch) round cake tin. Bake the small cakes for 10-12 minutes; the large cake for 30-35 minutes, until golden brown and firm to the touch. Turn out the large cake and cool on a wire rack. Remove paper cases.
2 Split the cake into 2 layers and sandwich together with honey. Place on a thin 20cm (8 inch) cake board; place the pillars on a larger board, about 36cm (14 inches) in diameter, and position the cake on top. Spread honey over the top and sides of the cake.
3 Roll out three quarters of the moulding icing to a 30cm (12 inch) circle and place over the cake, fluting the sides to form the folds of the tablecloth. Stick flowers around the edge, securing them with a little honey.
4 Place 4 small cakes upside down around the cake, then position another cake on each one. Spread the tops with honey and cover with moulding icing, for the seats. Decorate with sugar flowers. Cut a 2.5cm (1 inch) circle out of the remaining cake, using a pastry cutter or small glass. Brush with honey and cover with icing. Decorate with flowers.
5 Colour remaining moulding icing blue. Shape a plate and position in the centre of the table. Secure a blue icing band around the tiny iced cake and place on the plate; use this for candles. Shape 4 small plates, saucers and cups and place on the table. Paint a design on the plates and saucers, if desired, using blue colouring and a fine brush. *Serves 12.*

Farm Cake

Farm animals from the toy box add the final touch to this popular cake; scrub them well before positioning.

3-egg basic cake mixture
  (page 79)
ICING:
375g (12oz/2½ cups) icing
  sugar, sifted
185g (6oz) soft margarine
1 tablespoon milk
orange and green food
  colourings

2 tablespoons cocoa powder
1 tablespoon hot water
TO FINISH:
2 x 150g (5oz) boxes chocolate
  finger biscuits
120g (4oz) box chocolate
  matchsticks
1 strip angelica, cut into tiny
  pieces

1 Preheat the oven to 160C (325F/Gas 3). Turn the cake mixture into a greased and lined 33x23cm (13x9 inch) Swiss roll tin and smooth the top. Bake for 25-30 minutes, until golden brown and firm to the touch. Turn out, remove paper and cool on a wire rack.

2 To make the icing, beat together the icing sugar, margarine and milk in a bowl until light and fluffy. Transfer 1 tablespoon to a cup and colour orange. Blend the cocoa and water to a smooth paste. Transfer two thirds of the plain icing to another bowl and beat in the cocoa. Colour the remaining icing green.

3 Place the cake on a board and mark the top diagonally into 3 'fields'. Set aside 3 tablespoons green icing; spread the remainder over the centre field. Spread chocolate icing over the other fields; mark lines on one with a fork and swirl the other to resemble mud. Cover the sides of the cake with chocolate icing and press on finger biscuits.

4 Cut the matchsticks into short lengths and position between the fields for fencing. Using green icing and a star nozzle, pipe lettuces over the forked field. With a small plain nozzle, pipe in rows of seedlings. Use orange icing to pipe dots for carrots; position angelica for stalks. Place sheep and ducklings in the green field and pigs in the mud. *Serves 15.*

Wigwam Cake

3-egg basic cake mixture
  (page 79)
CHOCOLATE ICING:
1 tablespoon cocoa powder
1 tablespoon hot water
375g (12oz/2¼ cups) icing
  sugar, sifted
185g (6oz) soft margarine
GLACÉ ICING:
185g (6oz/1 cup) icing sugar,
  sifted

1½ tablespoons hot water
pink, yellow and green food
  colourings
TO FINISH:
30g (1oz) plain (dark) chocolate,
  melted
6 chocolate finger biscuits
4 chocolate matchsticks
1 chocolate gold coin

1 Preheat the oven to 160C (325F/Gas 3). Grease and base line a 470ml (15 fl oz/ 2 cup) and a 940ml (30 fl oz/3¾ cup) pudding basin. Two-thirds fill each basin with cake mixture and bake the small cake for 25 minutes, the larger one for 35-40 minutes, or until golden brown and firm to the touch. Turn out and cool on a wire rack.

2 To make the chocolate icing, blend the cocoa powder and water to a smooth paste in a mixing bowl. Add the icing sugar and margarine and beat until light and fluffy.

3 Split each cake in half horizontally and sandwich together with icing. Place the larger cake on a plate or cake board and spread the top with icing. Position the small cake on top. Trim the sides to form a smooth cone shape. Spread remaining icing smoothly over the top and sides.

4 Put the melted chocolate into a piping bag fitted with a small plain nozzle and pipe a chocolate door onto the cake, then pipe seams and stitches all over the wigwam.

5 For the glacé icing, mix icing sugar and hot water until smooth. Divide between 3 bowls and colour pink, yellow and green. Place in greaseproof piping bags and snip off the ends. Pipe zig-zag lines, dots and hieroglyphs on the wigwam.

6 Press finger biscuits into the top of the wigwam. Arrange a pile of chocolate matchstick logs alongside and place a gold coin over the door. *Serves 15.*

Swimming Pool

6-egg basic cake mixture
  (page 79)
4 tablespoons apricot jam,
  warmed
SOFT ICING:
250g (8oz/1½ cups) icing sugar,
  sifted
125g (4oz) soft margarine
1 tablespoon milk
blue food colouring

TO FINISH:
1 quantity moulding icing
(page 79)
yellow and red food colouring
1 crunchy oat bar
2-3 cocktail umbrellas
2-3 marshmallows
1 strip liquorice
12-15 jelly babies

1 Preheat the oven to 160C (325F/Gas 3). Turn the cake mixture into a greased and base lined 28cm (11 inch) square cake tin and smooth the top. Bake for 35-40 minutes, until golden brown and firm. Leave in the tin for 5 minutes, then turn out and cool on a wire rack.

2 To make the soft icing, beat together the icing sugar, margarine and milk in a bowl for 2-3 minutes, until light and fluffy. Set aside 2 tablespoons; colour remainder blue.

3 Cut four 1cm (½ inch) wide slices from one side of the cake. Stick the slices, cut side down, on the top edges of the cake, using jam and trimming to fit; reserve trimmings. Spread jam over the edges and sides of the cake. Set aside 125g (4oz) moulding icing. Roll out the rest and use to cover the sides of the pool, trimming to fit; reserve trimmings, Mark the icing into squares to make tiles. Spread the blue icing in the 'pool'.

4 Colour half the reserved moulding icing yellow; roll out and use to cover the crunchy bar. Attach to the side of the pool with soft icing for the diving board. Colour the plain moulding icing red. Form a slide from cake trimmings, cover with red icing and position on cake. Use leftover moulding icing to make towels, beach balls, etc; stick cocktail umbrellas into marshmallows for parasols, and use the liquorice to mark a swimming lane. Position jelly babies on poolside and in water. Serves 25.

Superstar Cake

A star theme is an easy one to follow through. Stick silver stars onto plates and beakers and make star-shaped labels for guests. Play musical stars – with large paper stars – as a variation of musical chairs.

6-egg basic cake mixture
  (page 79), flavoured with
  grated rind of 2 oranges
185g (6oz/½ cup) apricot jam,
  warmed
2 x quantity moulding icing
  (page 79)

DECORATION:
185g (6oz/1 cup) icing sugar
  sifted
4-6 teaspoons hot water
red food colouring
silver balls
silver ribbon

1 Preheat the oven to 160C (325F/Gas 3). Turn the cake mixture into a greased and base lined 28cm (11 inch) square cake tin and smooth the top. Bake for 35-40 minutes, until golden brown and firm. Leave in the tin for 5 minutes, then turn out and cool on a wire rack.

2 Place the cake on a 38x30cm (15x12 inch) board and cut out a triangle from the centre of the top edge to the bottom 2 corners. Reassemble the 2 pieces from either side as a second triangle and place over the uncut triangle, moving it until you have a balanced star shape. Cut out and remove the centre of the top triangle, to give a flat star. Stick the parts together with jam and spread jam over the top and sides.

3 Roll out moulding icing thinly and use to cover the cake pressing the icing onto the sides and trimming off excess.

4 Blend the icing sugar and water to a smooth icing. Place three quarters in a piping bag fitted with a small star nozzle and pipe stars around the top edge of the cake. Place a silver ball on each star. Using a small plain nozzle pipe the child's name in the centre, and a few star designs around the name.

5 Colour the remaining icing red and over-pipe the name. Apply silver balls to the designs. Attach a silver ribbon to the sides, with a little icing. *Serves 25.*

Treasure Chest

This appealing cake is one of the simplest of all to make and the children will love to help stick on the jewels.

*3-egg basic cake mixture
     (page 79)
2 tablespoon cocoa powder
2 tablespoons boiling water
ICING:
185g (6oz/1 cup) icing sugar,
     sifted
90g (3oz) soft margarine*

*TO FINISH:
gold and silver chocolate coins
chocolate eggs
strings of edible beads
fruit jellies
liquorice straps
silver and multicoloured balls
small jelly sweets*

1 Preheat the oven to 160C (325F/Gas 3). Blend the cocoa powder to a smooth paste with the boiling water. Add half to the cake mixture, and mix well. Turn into a greased and lined 1kg (2lb) loaf tin and smooth the top. Bake for 45-55 minutes, until golden brown and firm to the touch. Cool in the tin for 5 minutes, then turn out and cool on a wire rack.
2 To make the icing, beat together the icing sugar, margarine and reserved cocoa mixture in a bowl until light and fluffy. Using a sharp knife, slice off the top third of the cake for the lid. Place the base on a cake board and spread the top and sides with icing, marking the sides with a fork.
3 Spread icing over the top and sides of the lid and mark with a fork. Pile the chocolate coins, chocolate eggs, edible beads and fruit jellies onto the base of the cake and place the treasure chest lid on top as if half open. Position 2 pieces of liquorice over the back of the lid and base for the hinges.
4 Using tweezers, spell out the child's name in multi-coloured balls on top of the chest. Place small jelly sweets and coloured balls along the sides. *Serves 10-12.*

Bumble Bee Cake

*3-egg basic cake mixture
(page 79)*
2 tablespoon cocoa powder
2 tablespoons hot water
grated rind of ½ orange
orange food colouring
ICING:
*375g (12oz/2¼ cups) icing
sugar, sifted*

185g (6oz) soft margarine
1 tablespoon orange juice
TO FINISH:
4 fan-shaped wafers
4 liquorice strips
2 round sweets

1 Preheat the oven to 160C (325F/Gas 3). Grease and base line a 470ml (15 fl oz/2 cup) and a 940ml (30 fl oz/3¾ cup) pudding basin. Blend the cocoa powder to a smooth paste with the hot water. Put half the cake mixture into another bowl and mix in half the cocoa paste. Stir the orange rind and a few drops of orange food colouring into the plain mixture.

2 Two-thirds fill the basins with alternate spoonfuls of the mixtures. Stir with a fine skewer. Smooth the tops and bake the small cake for 25 minutes, the large one for 35-40 minutes. Turn out and cool on a wire rack.

3 To make the icing, beat together the icing sugar, margarine and orange juice in a bowl for 2-3 minutes, until light and fluffy. Transfer half to another bowl and beat in the reserved cocoa mixture. Colour the other portion orange.

4 Split the cakes horizontally. Sandwich the cakes together with chocolate icing. Place them on a 30x23cm (12x9 inch) board, touching each other.

5 Using piping bags fitted with star nozzles, pipe alternate bands of chocolate and orange icing stars across the cakes, beginning with a chocolate face at the front of the small cake and finishing with an orange tail at the end of the larger cake.

6 Place 2 wafers on each side of the body for wings. Cut six 10cm (4 inch) liquorice lengths and position on the body for legs. Cut a shorter piece and place at the front for the sting. Position round sweets on the face for eyes. *Serves 12-15.*

Cannon Cake

If you have enough time, make your own Swiss roll, using a 3-egg whisked sponge. Otherwise a ready-made one can be turned into an impressive cannon in next to no time!

1 large jam-filled Swiss roll
ICING:
1 tablespoon cocoa powder
1 tablespoon boiling water
125g (4oz/³/4 cup) icing sugar, sifted
60g (2oz) soft margarine

TO FINISH:
10 red liquorice strips
30g (1oz/¹/4 cup) chocolate sugar strands
2 chocolate fudge bars
2 chocolate mini Swiss rolls
2 large chocolate-coated biscuits
24 red sweets
4 chocolate silver coins
cannon balls (page 34)

1 To make the icing, blend the cocoa powder and water to a smooth paste. Place in a bowl with the icing sugar and margarine, and beat until light and fluffy. Set aside 2 tablespoons icing; spread the remainder over the sides and ends of the Swiss roll. Wrap all except one of the red liquorice strips closely around one end of the roll, trimming them to fit. Coat the rest of the roll with chocolate sugar strands.

2 Place a fudge bar in the middle of a 33x15cm (13x6 inch) board and centre the Swiss roll on it, supporting the front of the roll with the other fudge bar. Place the chocolate mini rolls on top of one another at the back of the cannon.

3 Attach the chocolate biscuits for wheels, using a little reserved icing. Secure a circle of red sweets around each wheel and at the upper end of the cannon. Place a silver coin in the centre of each circle.

4 Place a silver coin at the lower end of the cannon with the remaining liquorice strip leading from it, as a fuse. Position a pile of cannon balls next to the cannon. *Serves 8-10.*

Lion Cake

Transform a basic sponge cake into a magical lion with the minimum of time and effort.

*3-egg basic cake mixture
   (page 79), flavoured with
   1 teaspoon grated orange rind*
ICING:
*250g (8oz/1½ cups) icing sugar,
   sifted*
125g (4oz) soft margarine
1 tablespoon orange juice
orange food colouring

TO FINISH:
30g (1oz) plain (dark) chocolate,
2 white marshmallows
2 blue sweets
2 round wafer biscuits
*120g (4oz) box chocolate
   matchsticks*

1 Preheat the oven to 160C (325F/Gas 3). Half-fill 2 paper cake cases with mixture, then turn the remainder into a greased and base lined 23cm (9 inch) round cake tin. Smooth the tops. Bake the small cakes for 10-12 minutes; the larger one for 30-35 minutes until golden brown and firm to the touch. Turn the large cake out and cool on a wire rack. Remove the paper cases.

2 To make the icing, mix the icing sugar, margarine and orange juice in a bowl and beat until light and fluffy. Add enough colouring to give a rich orange tone.

3 Split the large cake into 2 layers and sandwich together with a little of the icing. Place on a cake board, positioning the small cakes on either side for the ears. Trim sides of large cake to shape face. Swirl the icing over the top and sides of the large cake, and on the top of the small cakes.

4 Using a piping bag fitted with a small plain tube, pipe a circle of chocolate for each eye, slightly larger than the marshmallows. Place the marshmallows on top and stick a sweet on each, using a little chocolate. Pipe chocolate in the centre of the ears, then pipe on eyebrows and nose. Position the biscuits as cheeks and pipe small chocolate dots on each.

5 Cut the chocolate matchsticks in half and place all around the lion's head for the mane. *Serves 12-15.*

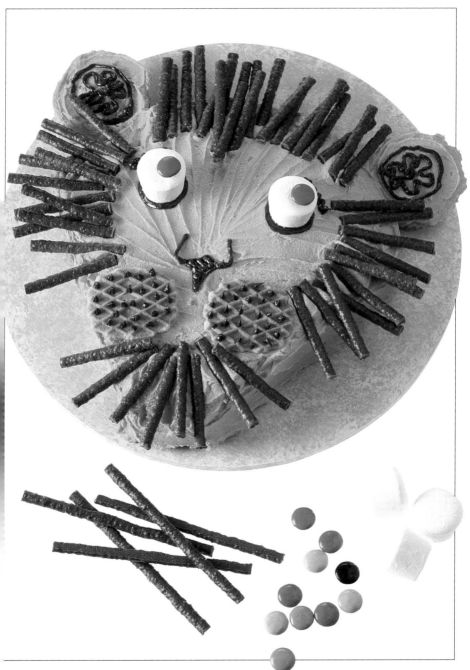

Clown Cake

3-egg basic cake mixture
  (page 79)
185g (6oz/½ cup) strawberry
  jam
1 quantity moulding icing
  (page 79)

yellow and red food colouring
1 metre spotted ribbon
  (3-4cm wide)
a little honey
2 liquorice strips
3 lollipops

1 Preheat the oven to 160C (325F/Gas 3). Turn the cake mixture into a greased and base lined 23cm (9 inch) round cake tin and smooth the top. Bake for 30-35 minutes, until golden brown. Turn out and cool on a wire rack.

2 Split the cake into 2 layers and sandwich together with two thirds of the jam. Place on a cake board and spread the remaining jam thinly over the top and sides.

3 Colour two thirds of the moulding icing with a few drops each of red and yellow colouring to give a flesh tone; knead until evenly coloured. Roll out and use to cover top and side of cake; trim off excess. Knead extra yellow colouring into the trimmings to make orange icing for the hair. Wrap in plastic wrap.

4 Position the ribbon around the cake and tie with a big floppy bow. Colour half the remaining icing red. Pull off a small piece about the size of a walnut and shape into a ball; press onto the cake for a nose. Divide the remaining red icing in half. Shape one piece into a sausage about 10cm (4 inches) long and flatten to form the hat brim. Roll the other half into a ball, then flatten into a D shape for the hat. Position the hat and brim together on the cake.

5 Roll out orange trimmings and cut into thin strips for hair. Attach to cake on either side of hat. Roll out half the white icing to a sausage, 13cm (5 inches) long, flatten and attach to the cake in a curve to form the mouth. Shape remaining white icing into 2 deep eyes and position.

6 Trim eyes and mouth with liquorice, securing with a little honey if necessary. Stick the lollipops into the hat.
Serves 12-15.

Helter Skelter Cake

6-egg basic cake mixture
(page 79)
red food colouring
SOFT ICING:
500g (1lb/3 cups) icing sugar,
sifted
250g (8oz) soft margarine
2 tablespoons milk
few drops of vanilla essence

TO FINISH:
½ quantity moulding icing
(page 79)
375g (12oz) fruit pastilles
6 ice cream wafers
2 small jelly sweets
4 jelly babies
3 lollipops

1 Preheat the oven to 160C (325F/Gas 3). Grease and base line a 470ml (15fl oz/2 cup), 940ml (30 fl oz/3¾ cup) and a 1.5 litre (50 fl oz/6 cup) pudding basin. Colour half the cake mixture pink. Two-thirds fill the basins with alternate spoonfuls of cake mixture. Stir together with a fine skewer. Smooth the tops of the cakes and bake the small cake for 25 minutes, medium cake for 35-40 minutes and the large one for 55-60 minutes. Turn out and cool on a wire rack.
2 To make the soft icing, beat all the ingredients together in a bowl for 2-3 minutes, until light and fluffy. Set aside.
3 Knead enough red colouring into the moulding icing to colour it deep red. Cover in plastic wrap; set aside.
4 Split the large cake into 3 layers and the others in half. Sandwich them together with soft icing, then assemble the cakes, on top of each other on a board, securing with icing. Trim to smooth sides. Swirl icing over the top and sides.
5 Roll the red icing to a thin sausage, 45cm (18 inches) long; press to flatten to a 3.5cm (1½ inch) wide strip. Starting at the top, position the strip round the cake to form a slide, pushing pastilles under the slide for support.
6 Cut two wafer doors and place one at the top of the slide and one at the base. Stick jelly sweet handles on each, using icing. Cut 'mats' from wafers. Attach 4 jelly babies to mats and stick on the slide. Place a pile of mats at the base. Stick pastilles around the top and base and around the cake above the slide. Press lollipops in the top. *Serves 25.*

Mini Train

Position the train around the birthday cake on the table. The children will be thrilled when they see their names on the carriages. Of course, the birthday child has the engine!

60g (2oz/¹/₃ cup) icing sugar,
sifted
2-3 teaspoons water
assorted liquorice sweets

12 chocolate-covered mini Swiss
rolls
jelly sweets
toffee-coated popcorn

1 Blend together the icing sugar and water until smooth. Place in a piping bag fitted with a small plain tube. To make the engine, cut 2 round liquorice sweets in half and attach to 1 mini roll with a little icing, to form wheels. Stick a round sweet on the front of the roll. Position a large square sweet, with a round one on top towards the back, for the engine cab. Stick a liquorice tube on the front of the engine for the funnel and put a piece of popcorn on top for smoke.
2 Use round liquorice sweets for the wheels of the other carriages, sticking them to the mini rolls with icing. Stick sweets on top of some, and popcorn on others, for coal. Pipe a child's name on each carriage, if you like.
3 Place the engine and carriages on the table and link them together with tube-shaped liquorice sweets. *Serves 12*.

NOTE: The mini train is illustrated on page 1.

Basic Cake Mixture

3 eggs
185g (6oz/1½ cups) self-raising
   flour

185g (6oz/¾ cup) caster sugar
185g (6oz) soft margarine
1½ teaspoons baking powder

Place all the ingredients in a bowl and beat with a wooden spoon until light and fluffy, about 2-3 minutes. Continue as directed in individual recipes.

FOR A 5-EGG CAKE: Use 315g (10oz/2½ cups) flour, 315g (10oz/1¼ cups) sugar, 315g (10oz) soft margarine and 2 teaspoons baking powder.

FOR A 6-EGG CAKE: Use 375g (12oz/3 cups) flour, 375g (12oz/1½ cups) sugar, 375g (12oz) soft margarine and 2 teaspoons baking powder.

Moulding Icing

1 egg white
1 rounded tablespoon liquid
   glucose

500g (1lb/3 cups) icing sugar,
   sifted

1 Place the egg white and glucose in a bowl and beat together lightly with a fork. Add the icing sugar gradually, beating with a wooden spoon until the icing is very stiff. Knead in the remaining icing sugar with your hands until a smooth silky ball is formed.
2 Continue kneading the dough on a surface sprinkled with icing sugar until it is no longer sticky. Wrap in plastic wrap and set aside until needed.

Index